TO STAND IN THE CROSS

ILLUSTRATIONS BY BABS GAILLARD

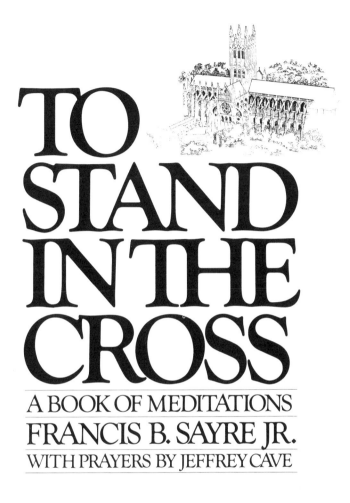

TO STAND IN THE CROSS

A BOOK OF MEDITATIONS

FRANCIS B. SAYRE JR.

WITH PRAYERS BY JEFFREY CAVE

A CROSSROAD BOOK

THE SEABURY PRESS • NEW YORK

Quotations from the Holy Scriptures are from The New English Bible, copyright
1961, 1970 by the Delegates of the Oxford University Press and the Syndics of the
Cambridge University Press.

1978
The Seabury Press, 815 Second Avenue, New York, N.Y. 10017

Printed in the United States of America

Library of Congress Cataloging in Publication Data

Sayre, Francis B   To stand in the cross.
"A Crossroad book."
1. Good Friday sermons. 2. Protestant Episcopal Church in the U.S.A.—
Sermons. 3. Sermons, American. I. Title.
BV95.S29   252'.62   77-13259   ISBN 0-8164-0380-5

LIST OF ILLUSTRATIONS

INTRODUCTION

On the highest hill in our nation's capital stands a cross. Flying into the city from east or west, north or south, the cruciform shape of Washington National Cathedral looms large over the city. The dean of the cathedral, the Very Reverend Francis B. Sayre Jr., has lived and worked in the shadow of that cross for twenty-six years.

Throughout the cathedral there are constant reminders of the birth, death and resurrection of Our Lord Jesus Christ and from these images in stone and glass the dean has created a series of meditations on the happenings of Good Friday.

Entering the cathedral from its western doors, one looks down the lengthy aisle and sees lowering over the crossing the rood beam with its carved wooden crucifix. Behind the rood beam, in gleaming stone, is the Christus Majestus, the risen Lord in majesty. There one is faced with the eternal mystery of Good Friday and Easter. It is with this basic aspect of our Christian heritage that Dean Sayre has grappled in these meditations.

As we enter the Lenten period, a time for study and thought, let us consider the significance of a church built in the shape of a cross in a city which many consider the crossroads of the world. Let us consider the beauty of that great church, signifying the beauty which Christ in his agony in Gethsemane knew he must leave behind. "The more life is radiant, the sadder is the grief of death," says Dean Sayre. And yet, we know that the sorrow we experience is transfigured in the exultant joy of Easter Day.

So, let us join together in a brief journey with the Gospels of Mark and John as our signposts and the dean as our guide. Let us go from Gethsemane to Golgotha, to the mystery of the empty tomb and beyond to the great revelation of Easter.

And as we go, let us give thanks for the gifts of God which have permitted us to create on Mount Saint Alban an edifice in which the worship of that triune God may be carried out in beauty, in dignity and in love.

John Maury Allin
Presiding Bishop

THE CROSS

Now the Festival of Passover and Unleavened Bread was only two days off; and the chief priests and the doctors of the law were trying to devise some cunning plan to seize him and put him to death. 'It must not be during the festival,' they said, 'or we should have rioting among the people.' (Mark 14:1–2)

Everyone in America knows about Broadway and Forty-Second Street—the most famous intersection in the land, unless it's Hollywood and Vine.

But nearly everybody in the whole world has heard of that much greater crossing, where the life of God intersects with the life of his children on earth. It is the Cross of Christ, in the shadow of which you and I are sitting on this Good Friday.

Here, flung upon this rise of ground, at the heart of our nation's life, is that very cross. It is the shape of this cathedral church, the shape of Christ's dying, his agony and our reproach; the utter fallibility of everything in this world which one day must perish, even the sacred things we cherish the most. But it is, too, the shape of our hope, recalling the place where God redeemed the death of his son, and forgave us for it and lifted us with him to a wholly new kind of life, which can never, never be taken away.

Look about this exquisite cathedral; you will find all these dimensions here. Here in the crossing intersects all the length and breadth of life. In medieval times cathedrals were quite literally marketplaces, the only open space in town, where people could transact their business. Even so, now come the crowding steps of thousands who have business to transact with each other or with their government. Here cross the lines of east and west and meet the paths of the human spirit in all its rich diversity. Here, as in the city around it, is found man's teeming rivalry, the coursing energy of his pride and purpose.

But then as rarely in the city, God adds a third dimension, giving body to these shadows. To the length and breadth of human affairs, he adds the height of Heaven; eternity thrust into the middle of time. A tower high above your heads proclaims "Gloria in Excel-

14

sis," its straight lines pierce this crossing vertically, down deep to the foundation roots in the earth below and its crown proclaims the final conquest of God's love, truth and life.

It is a new plane of existence that cuts across our little tracks, one that is beyond death itself, yet entered through it. It is beyond pain, and yet discovered there; beyond all defeat and betrayal, yet meeting us precisely there. This is the Cross of Christ in the midst of which we are standing, which he holds out to us, at that busy intersection where his life and ours are intertwined, where sometimes we see his body hanging and sometimes see only the bare wood, because he is no longer there, but risen indeed.

So in these three hours, when we wish to meditate upon these holy mysteries, let us take the great cross of this church and walk about in it in all its beauty, in all its poignancy, and let it speak to us. Each stone, each bit of glass in this place was born of someone's prayer; perhaps they will illumine our own prayers. For here, upon this hill, is the print of God. We have only to follow the track where he has trod.

Come, Lord Jesus, and stretch out your
    arms again upon the cross for us;
    bow down your head again for us,
and commit our spirits with thine unto your
    Father in heaven.
Bless us all with the sacred sign of the cross,
which was traced upon our brow at our bap-
    tism,
and which is builded up for all to see upon
    this holy mount.
May we all look to you and be saved,
and partake with you of the radiance and
    peace of the Father's everlasting halls,
where with thee and the holy spirit, he reigns
    in all eternity. Amen

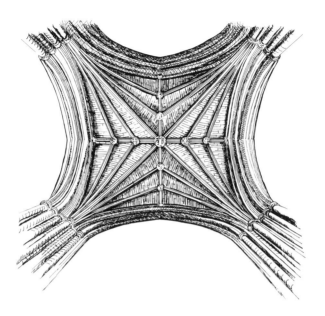

LOVE

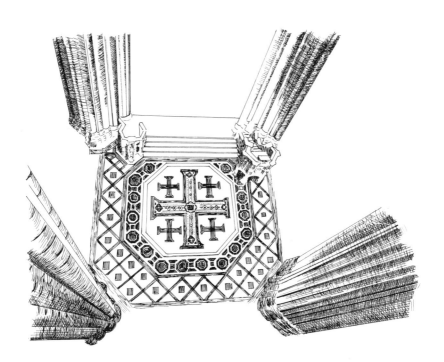

Jesus was at Bethany, in the house of Simon the leper. As he sat at table, a woman came in carrying a small bottle of very costly perfume, pure oil of nard. She broke it open and poured the oil over his head. Some of those present said to one another angrily, 'Why this waste? The perfume might have been sold for thirty pounds and the money given to the poor'; and they turned upon her with fury. But Jesus said, 'Let her alone. Why must you make trouble for her? It is a fine thing she has done for me. You have the poor among you always, and you can help them whenever you like; but you will not always have me.' (Mark 14:3–7)

"You will not always have me." With those searing words of Jesus, Mark begins his account of the Passion. Jesus sees what is ahead and Mark, the author, tries to help us understand it by describing the circumstance that clothed the words.

The master was in the house of a leper, Simon by name, having supper there. Was he a friend, this man of dread disease? Who dares to befriend the outcasts, the poor and the dirty of this world? Would you?

At any rate, there he was, sitting at table, in the little village of Bethany. One must suppose that it was a very ordinary scene in Jesus' life. But all of a sudden it became quite extraordinary! For a woman came in, quietly knelt down and, without a word, offered him the most precious gift she could contrive. "What is she doing?" cried the company, "wasting that costly ointment for no reason at all?" Only Jesus saw the wistful love, the inward fires of hope in that woman's heart, which she was moved to pour out, her gift, the gift of her soul to the one she already believed to be the Holy One of God. Maybe she was the first who ever believed that! But Jesus knew that love such as hers could never be fulfilled in this world until the soil around it be cleansed in suffering, winnowed from its selfishness, until the son of God endured the pain of death.

For is it not so in this world, even as it was in Simon's house, that sin forever besieges and imprisons the gentle flower of love? We're afraid to let it grow; until Christ transplants it to a realm that he could foresee, but of which the woman still could only dream.

"So let her be," he said to his hosts, "for the miracle is born in her already—that same miracle that I must finish for all the world, upon a cross. You will not always have me, but she knows that God is eternal and will not let love die."

How did she know that? How did she recognize the Christ? How? How does any person see the face of God reflected in the pool of his own yearning spirit? Surely the answer is because God first planted his love just there. And what God has planted, he will bring to bloom. Oh with what bated breath we await the blossom, along with that woman long ago.

Here, in this cathedral, is embedded the vision of this resurrection. You will not have noticed it; one never does. It's always hidden away in Simon's house, or an empty tomb or in a church like this. Thus, to take an example which you can see from where you sit, he who planned these four massive columns, here under the tower, wanted them to be like great trees. Reaching upward toward heaven, their branches are spread across the vaulting of the sky, each carved keystone a bloom of loveliness to the praise of our Redeemer.

If your spirit is thus lifted in the presence of these piers, then you should learn the secret of how the heavy stone is given the lightness of a flower. It lies in the fact that the columns are not perfectly vertical. If they were it would seem to us tiny people that those great heights were falling in upon us, all those tons of stone over our heads. But it is not so, for those columns are made to lean back ever so imperceptibly. Just a fraction of an inch every few feet compensates for the meanness of our little perspective, and lifts us up to a fresh dimension of life, instead of crushing our spirit to the ground.

Even so, by design of the great architect of all Creation, was one rude piece of wood laid across another in such fashion that Christ who had seemed to be merely a man turned out to be God. The world hardly seemed to notice it at all. Because, unlike that blessed woman, it was not looking. But there were a few heavy hearts that were given the lightness of a flower in the springtime.

Keep forever fresh in our hearts, O Lord,
the fragrance of your love;
yet in our delight of you
let us never turn away
from the stench of disease, or poverty or the
ugliness which is to you the very shape of
salvation.
Within the paradox of life,
keep us close to the paradox of the cross;
within the ironic turning of fate
let us trace the course of your design for us.
Keep us open to the needs of those who to us
are untouchable,
whether they be richer or poorer, more beautiful, seemingly grotesque or simply different—for the alabaster jar contains within it
the secret of your meaning for us,
our prophet, our priest and our king. Amen

When they reached a place called Gethsemane, he said to his disciples, 'Sit here while I Pray.' And he took Peter and James and John with him. Horror and dismay came over him, and he said to them, 'My heart is ready to break with grief; stop here, and stay awake.' Then he went forward a little, threw himself on the ground, and prayed that, if it were possible, this hour might pass him by. 'Abba, Father,' he said, 'all things are possible to thee; take this cup away from me. Yet not what I will, but what thou wilt.'

He came back and found them asleep; and he said to Peter, 'Asleep, Simon?' (Mark 14:32-37)

"Take this cup away from me. Yet not what I will, but what you will." Here, beneath the exquisite rose, the third great "eye" of this cathedral church, is perhaps the best place to ponder and understand Jesus' agony in Gethsemane garden. There he was surrounded by loveliness and peace. He knew it all must be torn from him. Horror and dismay came over him, the Bible says.

The more life is radiant, the sadder is the grief of death! In the glorious splendor of this western rose all creation glows, vibrant with God's handiwork. How turn one's eyes to face the darkness? "My heart," said Jesus, "is ready to break with grief." That was Gethsemane; he would have to leave the Earth he was born to love.

Look again at Rowan LeCompte's great rose and you will understand Christ's agony. "Let there be light" shouts the hub of the great wheel. "In the beginning God!" Coals of fire, infinity of blue! And like jewels around the rim, a multiplicity of forms gathered in the petaled tracery. Listen to the artist's list of what these forms might suggest to one who stood here in this garden of stone looking up at the twinkling light. The song of birds, at one o'clock, then moving clockwise, phases of the moon, the crystalline order, ebb and flow, at the bottom; ways through the wilderness, seed into flower, green islands, spiraling galaxies, branching development, and right at the top—the four elements of earth, air, fire and water. All the wondrous marvel of God's making is in that sparkling rainbow.

But now, close your eyes and measure Christ's sorrow in the darkness, when God's miracle no longer can be seen. Who murders that beautiful planet which is our island home? Who sullies the air and spoils the water? Who betrays the trust of children, many yet unborn? Who builds all those barren walls that shut men in and keep God out? "Were you there, when they crucified my Lord?"

Now, open your eyes once more, the light returns, but it is in a different place. On the columns of the nave you can perhaps see the little rainbows cast by prisms in the window. They move, they almost dance in the course of a whole day. They are in another spot than when you closed your eyes just now. And by these rays cast through the eye of crystals you are reminded that it is not the window itself that gives the light, but the Sun behind it— moving across the sky ninety-five million miles away.

O you who sorrow in the garden, is God really so eternally far away if his light, shining from the other side of the cross, can use it as a prism to dance upon the trees, and

come stealing into the darkness on our side
to give life to our death?

What gloom there is on Golgotha but what
radiance beyond—to pierce the blackness
with his will, not ours to be done.

Holy Father, Holy Son and Holy Spirit;
do you reflect upon us the lumines-
cence of your grace,
the plenitude of your power and the gift of
your love?
Bless with your goodness the filaments and
flickerings of light which bathe these holy
walls with the colors of your divine life.
May they betoken to us your presence, so
that inspired in the darkness of sin and
death we may still rise to be your creative
and redeeming society in a darkling world;
who lives and reigns one God, through end-
less ages. Amen

FREEDOM

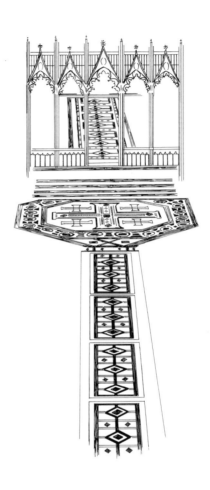

Then they seized him and held him fast.
Then they led Jesus away to the High
Priest's house, where the chief priests,
elders, and doctors of the law were all assembling. Peter followed him at a distance right
into the High Priest's courtyard; and there he
remained, sitting among the attendants,
warming himself at the fire.

The chief priests and the whole Council tried
to find some evidence against Jesus to warrant a death-sentence, but failed to find any.
Many gave false evidence against him, but
their statements did not tally. Some stood up
and gave false evidence against him to this
effect: 'We heard him say, "I will pull down
this temple, made with human hands, and in
three days I will build another, not made
with hands." ' But even on this point their
evidence did not agree.

Then the High Priest stood up in his place
and questioned Jesus: 'Have you no answer
to the charges that these witnesses bring
against you?' But he kept silence; he made no
reply. (Mark 14:46, 53–61)

But why a cross? Why must God choose such abject defeat as a vehicle for his forgiveness? An affront to the world, such a repelling disguise for omnipotence to wear! Was he toying with us, to squander so much love and trust upon that barren cross? What good was that? Why does the noblest and the best, no less than the most depraved, have to pass through death, before it can be redeemed? That's pretty hard for the world to take! For what does the world really know of death or want to know?

Maybe the answer to these conundrums is to be found in the High Priest's courtyard, after the arrest of Jesus. Shortly he would be before the judge in his tribunal. But what would the evidence be at the trial? One cannot help but be struck by the lack of unanimity among the accusers. The Bible twice records that the leading priests and members of the council could not get together on a case. It is said that "their statements did not tally, their evidence did not agree."

By this we recognize that same familiar race of humanity Jesus came to save forever wearing the badge of freedom God placed upon their brows in image of his own, but using that freedom to differ, to dispute, to build and tear down. Each man in his royal liberty is devoted to his own sacred perspective.

It is startling also to realize that if the witnesses against God could not agree, neither can our testimonials in his behalf. For how shall you describe a fathomless mystery? One man will swear to this and another to that. One has seen God's love, another his righteousness, still another has heard him in strange voices or found him among the rocks and quiet places.

Incorrigible in its variation is the human race, fashioned as it is after the infinitude of God. And this was the special heritage that Jesus could not violate! The only parameter of his mission was that he might not infringe upon the sovereign freedom of a single soul. He would have to win people; he could not coerce them.

So it was, as I imagine, when long before the end, Jesus plotted his lonely course in the wilderness, he decided upon a cross. He would seduce by utter love what he might not force, even by divine perogative. It was God's loving way, not ours.

This too is reflected in our cathedral—wondrous witness that it is! Have you remarked that the aisle in front of me is by no means straight? No, it curves imperceptibly, as Christ's body must have curved where it hung upon the cross. Thus, the great church has a moving sense of grace, rather than rigidity! If all were perfectly regular, mathematic in its precision, how stiff and Prussian would the line of columns be, repugnant psychologically to our liberty. But instead there is that graceful irregularity turning with love, rather than with law, toward the redeeming of the world.

"Gothic variations," they are called, the little individualities of each bay, each arch and aisle. The vaulting is not level, it climbs toward the west. The radius of the arches varies from bay to bay; no two arcades are alike.

God's Kingdom is made of grace, not geometry; and his love beguiling would rather die for us than take away the sacred birthright of our liberty!

Come Holy Spirit,
   the spark of divinity within,
   the leaping flame without,
the sacred gift of freedom,
the holy bond of community,
the inspiration of artist,
the curiosity of scientist,
the restraint of politician,
the eloquence of preacher,
the gentleness of good shepherd,
the grace of simplicity and
the complexity of the unfathomed universe.
Come Holy spirit, all this.
Help us to abandon ourselves to your guid-
   ance.
Help us to remain ourselves.
Help us to grow in your grace as did the
   Christ, who died a free man to make us
   free. Amen

TRUTH

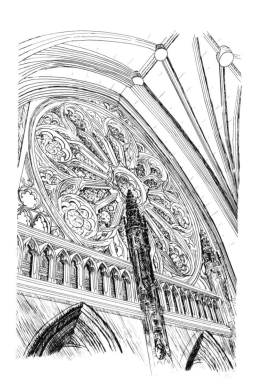

Pilate then went back into his head-
quarters and summoned Jesus. 'Are you
the king of the Jews?' he asked. Jesus
said, 'Is that your own idea, or have others
suggested it to you?' 'What! am I a Jew?' said
Pilate. 'Your own nation and their chief
priests have brought you before me. What
have you done?' Jesus replied, 'My kingdom
does not belong to this world. If it did, my
followers would be fighting to save me from
arrest by the Jews. My kingly authority
comes from elsewhere.' 'You are a king,
then?' said Pilate. Jesus answered, ' "King"
is your word. My task is to bear witness to
the truth. For this was I born; for this I came
into the world, and all who are not deaf to
truth listen to my voice.' Pilate said, 'What is
truth?' (John 18:33–38)

Christ, hanging there upon his cross, is vir-
tually alone—one fixed point in the swarm-
ing sea of humanity. I suppose it is always
so, when any man comes to die; we have finally to do it alone and all of us can understand the human pathos of that.

But there was a deeper, almost cosmic reason

why Jesus was so terribly alone, dying there between two thieves. You can see what that reason is, if you think of the confrontation of Pilate and Jesus at the trial. "Are you a King?" the governor challenges. "My kingly task is to bear witness to the truth," Jesus replies. "Ah, but what is truth?" Pilate asks.

And there the governor speaks for the whole world, for all the jostling company of human beings in all ages and climes. Who can be sure? Who can say with absolute certainty what is true or false, right or wrong? All, all is relative, and no matter how zealously we lay claim to the authority of our gods, still there are always ways of shading it. History is only the well where you will see your own face reflected. And truth has no more authority than your image of it.

In a world where that is the final analysis, where expediency must forever prevail above principle, there are no absolutes. A proclamation such as that of this cathedral's northern rose comes as an affront; a claim of outrageous pretension. For it declares the Last Judgment, a final standard from beyond this Earth by which everything is appraised and tested, even down to the most secret of your thoughts. There it is, like some great eye staring down from on high into the body of this church, where cross the crowded ways of life.

Look up there, the window is peopled with familiar images, houses built on rock, houses built on sand; gates of heaven above, lakes of fire below; all the more lurid imagery of the Christian faith; that kingly witness Jesus laid before Pilate. Truth, not our fragmentary and broken perception of it, but God's even as he made it, that was the royal gift he came to offer. And for that they killed him, not believing that there could be so plain a bridge betwixt ourselves and eternity. No man by himself can believe that, and that's why Jesus was utterly alone when he died.

And yet a king he was, bringing us a message from the other side. After he had risen we knew the answer to Pilate's question. Truth? Why truth is love—not neutrality, not hostility, but God's love for ever and ever. And by that love are all things tested, life and death and soul and body and mind and every day.

Like a star fixed forever at the center of the universe is the caring love of God, and we had better live up to that! It is the ultimate measure.

Let me tell you how Gothic vaulting is made, and then you'll understand how creation is put together! The very first stone to be set is the central one in each bay—the big Keystone called a boss. It's set on a stool in thin air just as creation was—*Ex Nihilo* there. You could call that the God-stone if you like, for it all begins with him. Then on arching forms of wood, the ribs are built, down to the column corners. They are like the basic laws of our environment. They hold it all up. And finally, in the triangles left by that cage of ribs, come all the little infill stones that could be likened to you and me. We fill in, with freedom, yet in consonance with our fellows, all the little holes of life.

As wonderfully as that is all God's handiwork contrived. He is at the heart, we at the branches. All is held together in that marriage of time and eternity that we call truth.

It was for that Christ died; that we might see both sides of that marvelous equation!

Come Lord Jesus into our doubting orbit with your claim of truth.
Confront us with our own uncertainties,
confirm your judgment of us—a judgment of love.
Sentence us to what we can barely stand—
more of your goodness and love.
Condemn us to ourselves, to our families, our neighbors and our friends,
and having done all that abandon us
again in the absence only of your love.
Your truth, Lord Christ, is hard to bear because it embarrasses us
where we feel most comfortable—with our favorite people,
in our favorite church, sampling tidbits of life and avoiding your monumental truth.
But, Lord Jesus, as you made it easy for Pilate and for the executioners, ruling as you did, not by coercion, but by winsome love, so make it easy for us to take your truth, to learn from it, to grow in it, to stick with it, to yearn for it, to proclaim it as from this holy hill, to all the world.
You, Lord, are the way, the truth and the life.
Amen

FAITH

After that, Jesus, aware that all had now come to its appointed end, said in fulfilment of Scripture, 'I thirst.' A jar stood there full of sour wine; so they soaked a sponge with the wine, fixed it on a javelin, and held it up to his lips. Having received the wine, he said, 'It is accomplished!' He bowed his head and gave up his spirit. (John 19:28–30)

How does one ever come by the courage of faith? To go beyond all you can possibly know, trusting truly the unknown! To venture one's life on what the world calls an absurdity; to reach across the bounds of finitude and grasp the hand you cannot see! Kierkegaard once said that faith is like swimming at the surface above seventy thousand fathoms of sea. You cannot see the bottom, you cannot see the shore, you just have to believe the water will hold you up and you will not drown.

And so it is an act of courage to confide your life to God, whom you have never seen, whose love you have not known half so well as his law, yet who requires of you a total allegiance of purpose and devotion even to the very risk of life itself.

I imagine that it was when he retreated to the wilderness, early in his life, that Jesus drew in his breath, the breath of his being, and decided to launch out upon the deep; forget himself, and serve God alone; dare to be eternity's man and not the prisoner of Earth's lovely blandishments. The Gospels are a record of his struggle to follow that resolve, and therefore of his manhood, in that he was not immune to temptations such as ours. He too had to fight! But that path leads inevitably to Golgotha, where we have followed him this Good Friday.

Some of you may have walked the sad trail marked out in Jerusalem, which Christ is said to have trod on his way to the cross. Via Dolorosa they call it. And you may have lifted your eyes to the green hills around about the city, and seen the sun shining upon the stones of Galilee, the bitter olive trees spinning their leaves in the breeze.

Then you may think of Jesus, his eyes steadfastly fixed upon a greater glory beyond. He must pass through that loveliness to a beauty more everlasting.

If, for a moment, you dare to walk with him, then peek through yonder doors of the transept. There, beyond the glass is the exquisite springtime of Washington, azalias and dogwood and magnolia, all manner of entrancing new birth to burst upon the senses. A band of young would-be gardeners have even transplanted a little snatch of spring into the cathedral itself over there in the flowers by the font (see page 33).

And as Jesus passed such happy landmarks of God, he must have been thinking too of the human lives he had seen God bring to blossom. The widow with her mite, the boy who gladly gave his loaf and fish, that the multitude might be fed. The woman that was a sinner, was it she who had poured the costly oil upon his head?

There they stand, these and others, in the niches of this south transept portal, just outside the door. Each had brought his treasure to Christ. But he would have to leave them now—and go on beyond.

So, at the last, all comes to climax upon the cross, as Jesus utters these last few words, "I thirst" and, bowing his head "It is accomplished." In that final moment just before he takes the fearsome leap across the chasm, his body holds him fast; he can still suffer the bitter cruelty that gives him vinegar for water in his agony.

Ah, that is the greatest act of faith that somehow knows a greater body on the other side where there is no bitterness or gall, but only the brightness of God's love. It is a thousand times more radiant even than the promise of spring at the dawn of the morning.

His faith—and ours!

God our Father,
you give to us your children precious gifts:
faith, hope and love.
The greatest of these is love,
but the way to love is through faith in your promises.
Grant us a measure of faith, made by you, not by us;

give us faith in your faithfulness;
faith in your forgiveness of our sin;
faith in your rectitude and justice;
faith in your kingdom, already come, and
coming still;
faith in the man Jesus, who does not separate
faith and hope and love, but is them all,
upon the cross.
Integrate our lives with the gift of yourself,
that your faith in us and our faith in ourselves may reflect your purposes;
and that we may act out our faith in loving
deeds,
and that our spiritual attitude may be always
one of hope. Amen

SPIRIT

At midday a darkness fell over the whole land, which lasted till three in the afternoon; and at three Jesus cried aloud, 'Eli, Eli, lema sabachthani?', which means, 'My God, my God, why hast thou forsaken me?' Some of the bystanders, on hearing this, said, 'Hark, he is calling Elijah.' A man ran and soaked a sponge in sour wine and held it to his lips on the end of a cane. 'Let us see', he said, 'if Elijah will come to take him down.' Then Jesus gave a loud cry and died. And the curtain of the temple was torn in two from top to bottom. And when the centurion who was standing opposite him saw how he died, he said, 'Truly this man was a son of God.' (Mark 15:33–39)

In the ancient abbeys and churches of Christendom, there was quite usually some kind of step or screen or both that divided the choir from the rest of the church. This screen was generally topped by what is called the rood beam, on which the crucifixion is always depicted. The word *rood* is simply the old English form of *rod* or *pole,* and refers to the wood on which Christ died.

It was always placed at the intersection of the cross, to suggest that it is the passage through the cross that separates the choir of angels, inside, from the crossway of the world where people meet outside. You cannot perceive Christ in his glory carved there over the high altar until you have first understood Christ in his suffering and sacrifice.

Thus, as chief iconographer for this cathedral, I can tell you that all the myriad carvings, all the windows and symbolic meanings embedded in this building, revolve around that lofty timber, to which we hardly ever lift our glance, which shows that awesome moment when Christ ceased to be man and began to be revealed as God!

High over your heads marches the long line of stones, called "bosses," a tenth of a mile from the great west doors to the apse. Carved upon them is the Nicene Creed, beginning with creation, heritage of all creatures and ending over the high altar, the resurrection of the body and the life everlasting. But that last is not the heritage of all, only of the tiny few who, having seen Christ die, were privileged to see the further dimension of his life and miraculously to share it with him.

So midway in that creed, the cross is the pinion between what we are given to know in the world and what we are given to know by faith. This is true also of the stained glass windows of this and many churches. Below the rood, to the west, they sing the song of saints, of prophets and servants and discipleship. But above the rood they tell of angels and heavenly visions, of a land undiscerned except through the prism of Christ's death and resurrection.

So beneath this rood, through the cross, we pass to a new frame of being. Here is the length and breadth of life—crossing here where you see the cross set into the floor. And above, vertically, is the third dimension of height, the great tower above, the foundations below. This is the dimension that gives body to life, God's glory, that keeps it from being utterly flat.

But the fourth dimension is beyond that cross; it is the dimension of the spirit. Invisible to the naked eye yet smoldering in the heart of faith, it is the mien of that holy spirit that Christ wears when he is risen.

Already, even before he dies, there is a hint of it. Judas had to point Jesus out to the soldiers sent to seize him, so hidden was his holiness beneath the plainness of every day!

How much more, after he is lifted from the cross, the mode of his appearance is one of the spirit. He is not recognized at once; he passes through fast-locked doors; he fills the nets at Galilee.

On the tympanum, outside that southern entrance, is carved the scene of the road to Emmaus. There Christ meets his sorrowing disciples. They do not know him, even though he opened the scriptures to their understanding, even though their hearts "burned within them." Not until he sat with them in the little inn and broke bread with them and dipped it in the wine. Not until then, did they enter into the body and blood of Christ. At last they knew what he meant when he told them, "Take up thy cross and follow me."

Keep our minds, O God, attuned to things unfathomable.

Keep our vision sharp but always aware of your imperceptible presence beyond the realm of sight.

Keep our hearts calm in the knowledge of love greater than we can ever receive or give.

Beyond the cross and the grave, for the Christ and for us, is resurrection-life;

the fourth dimension to our lives, perceived only by faith, and bestowed only by your grace.

Help us to believe, O God, that

Christ has died, Christ is risen, Christ will come again. Amen

THE MIRACLE

When the Sabbath was over, Mary of Magdala, Mary the mother of James, and Salome bought aromatic oils intending to go and anoint him; and very early on the Sunday morning, just after sunrise, they came to the tomb. They were wondering among themselves who would roll away the stone for them from the entrance to the tomb, when they looked up and saw that the stone, huge as it was, had been rolled back already. They went into the tomb, where they saw a youth sitting on the right-hand side, wearing a white robe; and they were dumbfounded. But he said to them, 'Fear nothing; you are looking for Jesus of Nazareth, who was crucified. He has been raised again; he is not here; look, there is the place where they laid him. But go and give this message to his disciples and Peter: "He is going on before you into Galilee; there you will see him, as he told you." ' Then they went out and ran away from the tomb, beside themselves with terror. They said nothing to anybody, for they were afraid. (Mark 16:1–8)

Let this cave, here under the pulpit, be for us the empty tomb to which came Mary of Magdala and Salome, with their aching, yearning hearts, early that quiet Sunday morning. Ancient is the ritual of sorrow, therapeutic the last work of anointing the body and sewing up the shroud. The soul must acquiesce in death's gentle sleep, and the round of life continue.

But lo, the stone is rolled away, the body gone, the tomb is empty save for a strange young man in robe of white. Could it be an angel who spoke to the women there?

To them it was the first inkling of God's eternal miracle. They were "dumbfounded," the Bible says. Who would not be so, if confronted with evidence that the dead were alive once more? They fled from the place, for they were afraid. And who would not be terrified if God had really brushed so close, upsetting every canon of credibility, turning the world upside down, raising a corpse from its grave indeed?

Poor sad women, they are all of us. Who can believe in miracles at all, let alone such a total violation of all that we know? If that empty tomb is really true, then no one on this earth can be sure of even his next breath, so mixed up must all meaning be!

That was Nicodemus' problem, remember? "How can a man be born again?" he had asked Jesus. "Except a man be born again he cannot enter the kingdom of God," was the master's reply. And now it had happened, right there, right in the orbit of those women's lives, and they didn't know what to make of it.

There is a beautiful image of this in a little statue in the outer aisle on the south. It is a beautiful statue of Joan of Arc (see page 9), just at the moment when God first calls her to wield a sword for him in France. How wonderfully the sculptor has caught that awesome instant when the miracle came to her. She listens eagerly with the whole attention of her soul, hand cupped to her ear. She hears the voices, yet how could such a miracle be? A young girl to wield the Lord's sword! But at that instant she, like Christ before, was born anew, body and soul, completely! She was the same, yet utterly, vibrantly but invisibly different!

Herein is the possibility of our believing in this empty tomb. For when once you behold Christ risen from his prison, marvelously you begin to see the miracle happening over and over again.

Take these panels carved above this tomb upon the pulpit. Here is Bede, that venerable old monk who, in the joy of the risen Christ within, dispelled the goblins and dread fears of ancient Britons in their primitive forest. What miracle is it that makes of one man a window of blessed relief for a whole tribe? And here is Stephen Langton, archbishop, who with his barons forced King John to Magna Carta, and so breached the brutal tyranny of man's near universal enslavement. There is Tyndale, who first put news of God's grace into the English tongue, so that common folk might read of God's miracle in Christ and in themselves. And up there in the pulpit a man named Martin Luther King preached the last sermon of his life on this planet. Who today will gainsay the miracle by which God may take a single man and change a nation?

To me it matters not whether you begin with

the miracles of Christ's resurrection, and by it unlock the mystery of all the other miracles, or whether you begin the other way around with the many miracles you find strewn across life, and see them all summed up in that empty tomb where the dead body was no more. Gather up all the fragments of Christ, put them together and that is where the body is gone.

For as St. Paul put it, "If ye then be risen with Christ, seek those things which are above, where Christ sitteth on the right hand of God" (Col. 3:1).

Jesus, who raised the dead to life,
Jesus, who restored the sight of the blind,
Jesus, who drove out the devils,
Jesus, who changed water into wine,
Jesus, who walked upon the sea,
Jesus, who rose from the dead—
Come to us, save us, show yourself to us,
    even now, Lord Jesus.
Take our broken lives and make them whole;

take our brutal injustice and rule among your
    people;
take our worries and our little bothersome
    sins and wipe them away;
redeem our lives, make them new, turn them
    to yourself;
where the scales shall fall from our eyes;
and our stale bread shall become your body,
your living presence in our midst.
Break through our tombs of fear and anxiety
    and be with us, a miracle even now.
Jesus, Jesus, Jesus. Amen

MYSTERY

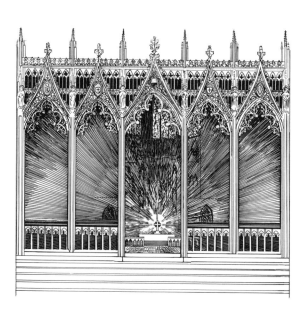

When he had risen from the dead early on Sunday morning he appeared first to Mary of Magdala, from whom he had formerly cast out seven devils. She went and carried the news to his mourning and sorrowful followers, but when they were told that he was alive and that she had seen him they did not believe it.

Later he appeared in a different guise to two of them as they were walking, on their way into the country. These also went and took the news to the others, but again no one believed them. (Mark 16:9–13)

Thomas was one of those who could not believe that Christ had risen. "Not until I see the print of the nails, and thrust my hand into his side," he declared. What a modern man he was! "Seeing is believing!" "Give me a microscope and let me test the thing!" And that was his definition of reality, a thing of the senses, of physics and mechanics and the material world around us. Good Thomas, he would have made a grand technician in an M.I.T. laboratory!

Then came Christ passing through a heavy door, closed and bolted in fear. He turns at once to our scientist friend, reading as he always did the inner secret within his heart. "Reach your finger here." "Touch with your hands my side." "Be not faithless, but believing."

That was the volcano in Thomas' life. Hot fire seemed to seize his soul. It was not what he had touched, but what had touched him! But there was no mistaking the reality in whose compelling presence he now stood. Reality is something much nearer, much deeper, much more immediate than he had dreamed. "My Lord, and my God," he finally acknowledged.

And then the Christ was gone, as mysteriously as he had come, incorporeal, incomprehensible, and yet more vivid and more vital than anything he had ever touched or known in his whole life.

For he is a mystery still, our risen Christ! And how could it be otherwise with God's inexhaustible life? No matter how much he reveals, much more remains hidden in the infinite realm of his being. So we must not expect any easy blueprints or children's catechism now. But rather the profound and unfolding shadows of a mystery.

How beautiful to know that they are not the shades of darkness, but rather the penumbra of love. God's forgiving, redeeming power which is seen upon that cross is at the heart of his Creation.

Can you see, from where you sit, the cross, glinting there at the high altar far away? It is lost in shadow, yes, wrapped in its distant mystery of time, of place and shrouded just now in memory of Christ.

But behind it, in the reredos behind the altar, are all those men and women in whom, like Thomas, the miracle was wrought. In all centuries, in all modes of Christendom, the great mystery of his resurrection changed their lives and, through them, the world. The miracle is veiled still in secret holiness, yet grafted into lives like yours and mine.

And this is what made the apostle shout—not just on Easter morning—"Not I liveth, but Christ liveth in me!"

O God our Father,
You promised unto Abraham
that he would be a father to a host of
nations;
that his descendants would be as the stars,
too many to number.
Behold your people.
Join us to the crucified one
in his embrace of all peoples,
and hear our cry
that all may be one,
as you and he are one with the Holy Spirit,
throughout all ages. Amen